Jimmy Stewart
and
His
Poems

Jimmy and His Poems

by Jimmy Stewart

Illustrations by Cheryl Gross

Crown Publishers, Inc.
New York

Published by Crown Publishers, Inc.,
201 East 50th Street, New York, New York 10022

CROWN is a trademark of Crown Publishers, Inc.
Manufactured in the United States of America

ISBN 0-517-57382-2

Design by Peter A. Davis

I'm sure I never said to myself, "Now, Jim—why don't you sit down and write a poem." It's still a mystery to me, but I think probably it's something that happened by accident—like a lot of things have happened in my life.

I have always envied people who kept diaries. This is a very logical way to keep events in your life on paper, instead of in your memory.

I have never been any good at keeping a diary. I was determined to keep one of my experiences in the war. But I failed completely, and when I got my footlocker back after returning from the service, I found my diary book with two entries: my first and second days in the service.

But getting back to poems. I think perhaps it was a desire on my part to write down an event that was unique and special in my life. The first time it happened I was in South America. I'll have to explain that.

Our very dear friends, Bess and Fran Johnson, arranged a trip for my wife, Gloria, and me to South America. It was essentially a fishing trip. We fished for marlin off the coast of Peru, and also fished the Chilean lakes for several days. This was wonderful, and we went fly-fishing for German brown trout that had been there for a long time. Gloria did the best and caught an eight-pound German brown. I was very proud of her and asked if we couldn't have the fish mounted.

Our guide, Gustavo Schwed, said we could do it in Argentina where we were bound. So, we put the fish on ice in the truck and started over the Andes to Argentina, which turned out to be quite a long trip.

During the trip the ice around the German brown trout melted, and the fish started to get a little high. For some reason we started to refer to the fish as George.

We finally arrived at our destination—a town called Junín de los Andes (the word *Junín* is pronounced *Who-neen*), which is a small place in western Argentina. But also, it was beside a wonderful trout stream filled with German brown and rainbow.

We checked into the hotel and were led up to the third floor with steps all the way. I tripped on the top step and fell down. I thought I was tired from the long drive.

The next day we were out in the trout stream and it was wonderful fishing. At the end of the day we returned to the hotel in Junín and started up the steps to our rooms. Then a strange thing happened. Every one of us who reached the top step tripped and fell down.

We spent one more day in Junín, and during that time I found out why we all tripped on the top step. I felt that I should record this in some way so I wouldn't forget it. As we left for our next stop in Argentina, I remember saying to Gloria—out of the clear blue sky—"The top step in the hotel in *Who-neen* is mean." It sort of surprised me that what I had just said rhymed. So, that night, at our next stop, I sat down and tried to tell the story of Junín and make it all rhyme. Here's what I came up with.

The Top Step in the Hotel in Junín

The top step in the hotel in Junín is mean.

Like the Devil is mean.

And it lies at the top of the other steps,

So quiet, so still, so serene.

But this top step has something quite special,

A very ingenious device:

It's half an inch higher than the other steps,

A whole inch to be more precise.

And it uses this inch as a weapon,

The guests of the place to harass:

For when you reach the third floor

of that hotel in Junín,

The top step trips you right on your ass.

Now I've had my share of knocks on the head,

I've felt enemy gunfire in war.

But if you want my opinion of what's really bad,

I'll be glad to give you the score.

Of all the degrading, inhuman, mean things,

That I in my life have yet seen,

The gross, most despicable one of them all

Is the top step in the hotel in Junín.

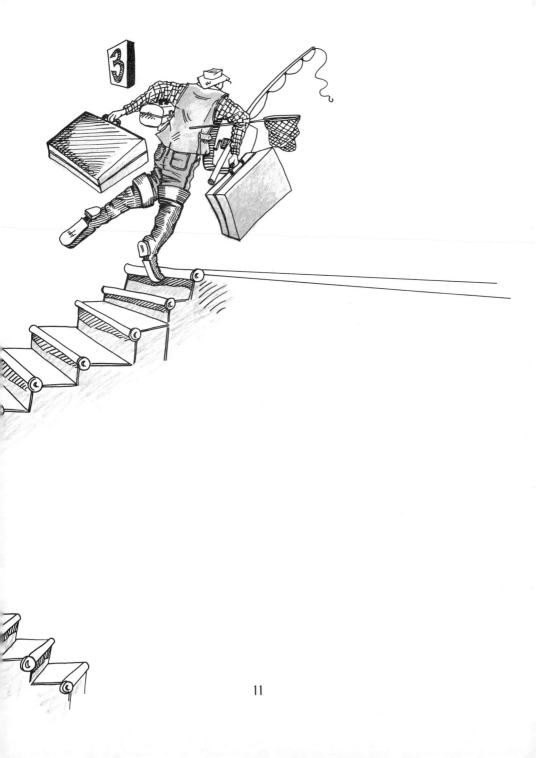

There is a beautiful mountain range just north of Nairobi, Kenya, in East Africa. It has beautiful forests, plains, rugged cliffs, and beautiful streams.

The wildlife there is amazing. There are elephant, rhino, and all the antelope—including kudi, eland—and especially bongo, a very rare and elusive animal.

Well, Gloria and I went to the Aberdares on a photographic safari. On this trip through the Aberdares we kept going higher and higher. When evening arrived we got to our camp, which was at six thousand feet. We had our dinner and sat around the campfire for a while; but I had a feeling that everybody realized that, in spite of the fire, it was cold—and getting colder. So, we all said goodnight and retired to our tents.

Getting into pajamas seemed a stupid thing to do because the minute I got under the blanket and my coat, I put on a sweater and some long underwear and some wool socks. This didn't solve the problem. I was cold. I couldn't remember when I'd been colder.

Then I asked myself: "Jim, how cold is it?" This got me thinking about cold places and I started writing things down in a notebook I had. Strangely enough, things started to rhyme—and this is what came out of it.

The Aberdares!

The North Pole's rather chilly,

Those who've been there all will tell.

There's lots of snow and lots of ice

And lots of wind as well.

An iceberg's really never warm

And takes a while to melt.

A snowball's not the hottest thing

That I have ever felt.

Siberia is never mild,

And never very nice.

They send a lot of people there,

And put them all on ice.

But then there's a place in Africa
That puts them all to shame.
They say Jack Frost was born here,
The Aberdare's its name.

They've never known the temperature,
Thermometers just fail,
For when exposed, the mercury
Just sinks below the scale.

It never ever snows here,
The snow it wouldn't dare,
Snow and ice aren't dummies,
It's cold in Aberdare!

As I lie here gasping in my tent,
The chill just numbs my spine.
Then suddenly a vision comes
That takes me back in time.

There's California sunshine
And I can breathe again,
A putting green—a fairway—
Relaxing in my den.

Then just as fast the vision leaves
No more sunshine, no more golf.
No need to wipe my tears away,
I simply break them off.

A frigid mist is moving in,
I've put on all my clothes.
There's not enough—the chill seeps in—
Is this the end? Who knows?

So gather your statistics,
Let all the facts be told.
Oh! Aberdare, you're beautiful,
But, Aberdare, you're cold.

Gloria and I had taken our daughters, Judy and Kelly, on photographic safaris in Kenya a couple of times, and we had lots of pictures. But I thought maybe it would be a good idea to get movies, too.

Eastman Kodak had just come out with a new 8mm camera with cassette-type film so you didn't have to thread it like you used to do. So, I got one for the twins and off we went to East Africa.

The twins took to the movie camera right away and, in no time, were expert in using it. The weather was good and there was good light, so we were all happy that we had a movie camera.

Then, one morning, we got up all rarin' to go, and we couldn't find the movie camera. We looked through every tent all around the camp, but it couldn't be found.

Then, suddenly, Judy called everybody around and said that she had left the camera in its leather case outside the tent the night before. Well, at that our guide, Bunny Ray, who was a former white hunter, told us to form a ring around the camp and move out from it.

After not too long, Judy yelled and we all went over to her. There was the movie camera—its lens torn off and lying in the grass—and huge teeth marks on the side of the camera, with the film torn out. Bunny just said it was a hyena, and that was that.

It was kind of quiet around the campfire that night, and I made a decision: I would write about what had happened and try to make it rhyme. I also decided to write it from the movie camera's point of view. Here's how it came out.

I'm a Movie Camera

I'm a movie camera, Instamatic is my name.

I'm Eastman's latest model,

   Super 8's my claim to fame.

I was on a shelf in Westwood

   when an actor purchased me

And took me home to 918 in Hills the Beverly.

I remember well the "Ohs" and "Ahs"

When out of my box I was taken.

I am a present to the actor's girls,

If I am not mistaken.

The actor read my handbook

And explained me to the twins.

They seemed to understand me

And expressed it with wide grins.

And soon I comprehended

What my mission was to be.

I'm to photograph the animals

In Kenya 'cross the sea.

They put me in a leather case

Of rather old design,

I wish it was a new one

But this one will be fine.

Then one day I found myself

Beneath a curious chair,

We were on our way to Africa

And were flying through the air.

A few days in Nairobi,

Then they put me in a car,

And we journeyed to the jungle camp

Which seemed to me quite far.

And then the action started

In the jungle all day long,

There was lots of picture taking

And the light was good and strong.

And then began a wondrous time—

The film we did expose.

We got the mighty lion

And right up to a tommy's nose.

But then there came the highlight

In a leopard blind one day,

And Kelly took a picture

As the leopard stalked its prey.

That night they praised

    the camera work

And I just burst with pride,

But if they like my work so much,

Why'd they leave me here outside?

A midnight wind came through the case

And chilled me to the core,

And also there were noises

That I hadn't heard before.

Then suddenly there was a tug

Upon the leather case,

As wind whipped 'cross the campsite

We were dragged across the place.

And through the grass it dragged us,

A dozen yards or so,

And then we stopped quite suddenly

And we waited—I don't know.

It came at once when with a snarl,

White fangs tore off the case

And left me lying in the grass,

This monster now to face.

It was indeed a monster

And its yellow eyes did glare

With viciousness upon me,

Almost more than I could bear.

Its slobbering jaws clamped down on me

If I could only shout—

It picked me up and shook me

And then it spit me out.

Judy found me after dawn,

As moisture filled the air.

I felt sorry as she sadly looked

As I was lying there.

The actor didn't say much,

He just shook his head and frowned.

As bit by bit they picked

Their Instamatic off the ground.

There really wasn't much to say

As you could plainly see.

It seems that a hyena

Tried to make a meal of me.

And so I'm all in pieces

My career is ended now,

I don't know what the future holds

It matters not somehow.

I hope the twins will think of me—

I hope the thoughts are good.

I'm just a movie camera

And I did the best I could.

When I was a kid I had a dog named Bounce. As I remember, he followed me home from school one day. Nobody in town claimed him, and my father said I could keep him.

Bounce wasn't allowed in the house very much, so my father helped me build a little house for him out in the backyard. The dog seemed to like that fine.

The next summer, while I was at Scout camp, Bounce was killed. My family didn't tell me about it until I got home, and I cried. I missed Bounce. For some reason I didn't look around for another dog. Maybe it was because of all the other things that were happening: school, and the Boy Scouts, and working in my father's store. It was sort of a busy time.

As time went on—with prep school and getting into college (that was a close call)—I just didn't give much thought to dogs; although I did remember the good days with Bounce every once in a while.

Then, after college and my time on the New York stage, and my first years in Hollywood, I didn't seem to have time for a dog. Then came the war, and I don't remember even seeing a dog for those four years. After the war and working to get started back in the movies, I had my hands full.

Then I married Gloria, and a whole lot of changes took place. When I married her, Gloria had a fine German shepherd that she was devoted to. His name was Bello. His complete devotion to Gloria was a wonderful thing to see. Bello, more or less, just put up with me for a while. Slowly, though, we got to know each other and things were fine.

Gloria taught me something I'd never known. That is, that you don't just have to have a dog around as a pet or a watchdog. You and the dog can become friends.

Bello became part of the family. He lived to a ripe old age, and we all were sad when he died. Gloria had another shepherd picked out, so after Bello came Pax—a fine young German shepherd. We all liked him, and he fit into the family very well. But Pax started having health problems soon after he arrived, and in a matter of four months we lost him.

In our search for another dog, Gloria decided on a change of breed. Although I think she will always love the German shepherd most, she brought a golden retriever into the family. His name was Simba and he made a hit with all of us. Simba was a very quiet, well-behaved dog. But we all felt that it would be good for him to have a companion. So along came a ten-month-old golden retriever named Beau.

Beau was a fine-looking young pup, but we soon found out we had a problem. Beau was on the wild side. He tried to bite holes in furniture. He dug huge holes in our lawn. When our neighbor knocked a tennis ball into our yard, he would go after the ball and bury it. Then, two days later he would dig it up and eat it. He bit people, including me. We all tried to calm him down, but he had his own ideas.

Through all this, I found myself getting closer to Beau for some reason. Maybe it was because after he had torn a hole in a sofa he would come to me to apologize. And through it all Beau and I became friends. After about a year, Beau quieted down a lot and we became better friends than ever.

Then it happened, I was making a picture on location in Arizona, and one night our veterinarian, Dr. Keagy, called me and told me that Beau was very sick and he was afraid he couldn't save him. I got the next two days off and flew home. Gloria and the kids were very quiet, and even Simba—who was now called "the old one"—seemed to be worried.

I went down to Dr. Keagy's office, and when I saw Beau I don't think he recognized me. He seemed to have trouble breathing. Dr. Keagy said he was in pain. After some time with him, I decided to take the doctor's advice and have Beau put to sleep.

I could hardly see to drive home because of the tears in my eyes, but I decided right then and there that I would write about my friend Beau and try to make it rhyme. It came out like this.

Beau

He never came to me when I would call

Unless I had a tennis ball,

Or he felt like it,

But mostly he didn't come at all.

When he was young

He never learned to heel

Or sit or stay,

He did things his way.

Discipline was not his bag

But when you were with him things sure didn't drag.

He'd dig up a rosebush just to spite me,

And when I'd grab him, he'd turn and bite me.

He bit lots of folks from day to day,

The delivery boy was his favorite prey.

The gas man wouldn't read our meter,

He said we owned a real man-eater.

He set the house on fire

But the story's long to tell.

Suffice it to say that he survived

And the house survived as well.

On the evening walks, and Gloria took him,

He was always first out the door.

The Old One and I brought up the rear

Because our bones were sore.

He would charge up the street with Mom hanging on,

What a beautiful pair they were!

And if it was still light and the tourists were out,

They created a bit of a stir.

But every once in a while, he would stop in his tracks

And with a frown on his face look around.

It was just to make sure that the Old One was there

And would follow him where he was bound.

We are early-to-bedders at our house—

I guess I'm the first to retire.

And as I'd leave the room he'd look at me

And get up from his place by the fire.

He knew where the tennis balls were upstairs,

And I'd give him one for a while.

He would push it under the bed with his nose

And I'd fish it out with a smile.

And before very long

He'd tire of the ball

And be asleep in his corner

In no time at all.

And there were nights when I'd feel him

Climb upon our bed

And lie between us,

And I'd pat his head.

And there were nights when I'd feel this *stare*

And I'd wake up and he'd be sitting there

And I'd reach out my hand and stroke his hair.

And sometimes I'd feel him sigh

  and I think I know the reason why.

He would wake up at night

And he would have this *fear*

Of the dark, of life, of lots of things,

And he'd be glad to have me near.

And now he's dead.

And there are nights when I think I feel him

Climb upon our bed and lie between us,

And I pat his head.

And there are nights when I think

I feel that stare

And I reach out my hand to stroke his hair,

But he's not there.

Oh, how I wish that wasn't so,

I'll always love a dog named Beau.